Explore the World of
Forces of Nature

Text by Anita Ganeri

Illustrated by Mike Saunders

A GOLDEN BOOK • NEW YORK

Western Publishing Company, Inc., Racine, Wisconsin 53404

Contents

How did Ayers Rock get its shape?
Ayers Rock in Australia is a huge oval block of red sandstone. It stands about 1,150 feet high and measures five miles around its base. Ayers Rock is all that remains of a huge mass of sandstone that once covered the area. It has been worn into its present shape by the wind and rain. The Aborigine people call it Uluru, which means "great pebble."

How did mountains form?

The outer shell of the earth is divided up into large pieces, called plates. Long chains of jagged mountains form when two plates crash into each other. The layers of rock buckle and are pushed together like an accordion to form fold mountains.

The Himalayas are many miles inland from the sea, but millions of years ago they formed part of the sea floor. Less than forty-five million years ago the Indian plate crashed into the Asian plate pushing up the highest mountain range in the world.

More about mountains

Block faulting is another way in which mountains are built. Block mountains are huge slabs of rock squeezed up between two cracks, or faults, in the earth's crust. Such mountains, which include the Sierra Nevada in California, have flatter tops than fold mountains.

The Andes of South America were once the home of a group of American Indians called the Incas. In the sixteenth century they built a huge city at Machu Picchu, and survived by growing crops on terraces on the mountainside. The city lay in ruins after the Inca Empire fell in the 1530s.

In 1951 "yeti" footprints were photographed in the Himalayas, but no one can prove that these shaggy, apelike creatures really exist. Many people claim to have seen yetis and similar creatures, called Bigfoot or Sasquatch, in North America. These may, in fact, have been brown bears.

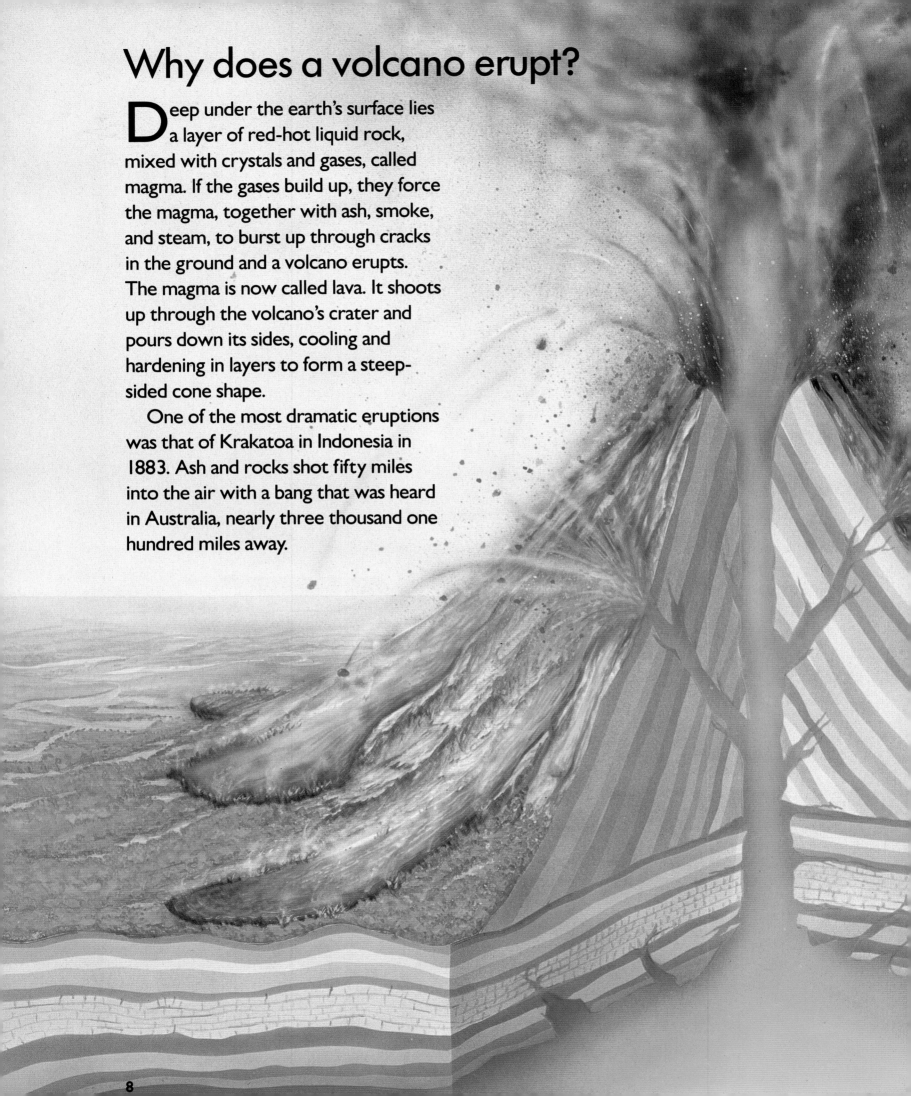

Why does a volcano erupt?

Deep under the earth's surface lies a layer of red-hot liquid rock, mixed with crystals and gases, called magma. If the gases build up, they force the magma, together with ash, smoke, and steam, to burst up through cracks in the ground and a volcano erupts. The magma is now called lava. It shoots up through the volcano's crater and pours down its sides, cooling and hardening in layers to form a steep-sided cone shape.

One of the most dramatic eruptions was that of Krakatoa in Indonesia in 1883. Ash and rocks shot fifty miles into the air with a bang that was heard in Australia, nearly three thousand one hundred miles away.

More about volcanoes

In A.D. 79 Mount Vesuvius in Italy erupted, covering the nearby town of Pompeii with thick ash. Thousands of people and animals died and their bodies left imprints in the ash. Many years later, archaeologists made plaster casts of these hollows.

Volcanoes that do not erupt anymore are called extinct. The chapel of Saint-Michel-d'Aiguilhe stands on an ancient extinct volcano near the town of Le Puy in France. Its eleventh-century builders had to carry their tools and materials 259 feet up to the top of the cone.

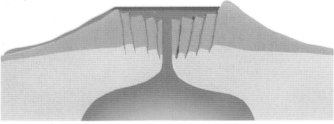

Volcanoes such as those in Hawaii erupt from several vents or holes. They are called shield volcanoes. The lava from these volcanoes is quite runny and thin. It bubbles up over the rim of the crater and flows a long way before hardening, so the volcano is not cone-shaped.

Where do geysers blow?

In places where there were once many volcanoes, the rocks below the earth are still very hot. They heat any groundwater until it is so hot that it bursts up through holes in the earth's surface. These scalding fountains of water and steam are called geysers. In some places, jets of steam alone shoot up from holes in the ground called fumaroles, or "fume holes."

One of the most famous geysers is Old Faithful in Yellowstone National Park. For over one hundred years it has gushed up regularly for a few minutes every thirty to ninety minutes.

The story of the earth

How was the earth formed?
Scientists think that the universe formed about twenty billion years ago. A huge explosion, called the "Big Bang," scattered hot gases and dust far out into space.

We do not know for sure how the earth and the other planets of the solar system were formed. An educated guess is that a cloud of gas and dust was pulled together by the force of gravity. As it whirled around, small particles bumped into one another to form bigger particles until, eventually, the planets were formed. The earth was born 4.6 billion years ago. The heaviest materials, such as iron and nickel, sank to form the earth's core. On the surface, the gases cooled to form rocks.

What did the early earth look like?
There were no plants or animals on the early earth, just volcanoes and bare rock. Water vapor rose from the volcanoes to form huge storm clouds, and torrential rain fell to form the first seas. These were very hot and as acidic as vinegar.

What are the continents?
Seven large plates and some smaller ones form the continents and ocean floors. About two hundred million years ago all the continents were joined as one huge landmass. But the moving plates split up and slowly formed the continents of today.

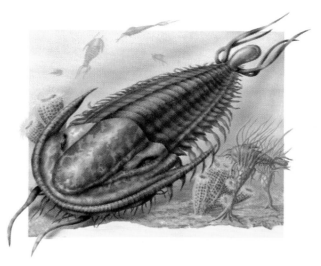

What were trilobites?
Trilobites lived from 570 to 230 million years ago in the prehistoric seas. They looked like horseshoe crabs with hard outer coverings. As they swam or crawled along the sea floor, they sifted the sand for food and hunted other sea creatures.

What were the early forests like?
About three hundred million years ago great swampy forests covered the earth. They contained huge club mosses, giant ferns, and early amphibians.

How long ago did the dinosaurs live?
The dinosaurs, or "terrible lizards," ruled the earth from two hundred million to sixty-five million years ago. The most ferocious was *Tyrannosaurus rex*.

How long will the earth last?
In about five billion years, scientists think the sun will have used up all its energy and will begin to die. The sun is a star. When most stars die, they swell up, and when the sun swells up, it will melt and destroy the earth.

What is the Great Rift Valley?

As the plates of the earth slowly move, they change the shape of the landscape. When two plates move away from each other, huge cracks, called faults, form. Sometimes a block of land between faults sinks, creating a long, narrow valley. This is called a rift valley.

The Great Rift Valley in East Africa is the longest rift valley on earth. As the valley formed, the earth's movement triggered off many volcanoes. These created great mountains such as Mount Kenya and Mount Kilimanjaro.

More about the Great Rift Valley

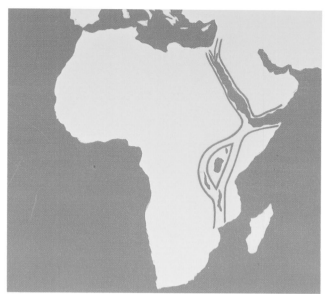

The Great Rift Valley stretches for three thousand miles from Jordan down to Mozambique. It is thirty to forty miles wide. The plates on either side of the valley are still moving apart very slowly. In fifty million years the valley may have widened so much that East Africa will be split apart from the rest of Africa.

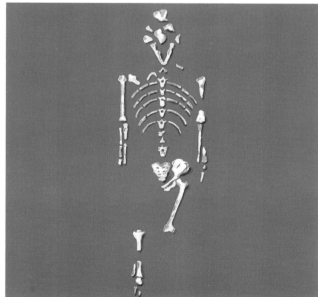

So far, Africa is the only place where remains of our earliest humanlike ancestors (who lived before human beings) have been found. The most complete skeleton yet found was discovered in part of the Great Rift Valley in Ethiopia. The three-million-year-old skeleton was nicknamed Lucy.

How do glaciers flow?

Glaciers start life high up in mountains, where layers of snow pack together to form ice. As more ice collects, its weight pushes the glacier downhill. Some glaciers creep along at a few inches a day, but some flow at more than eighty-two feet a day. The world's longest glacier, the Lambert Glacier in Antarctica, is three hundred and twenty miles long. Loose stones trapped beneath the glacier grind the mountain into sharp peaks and valleys.

More about glaciers

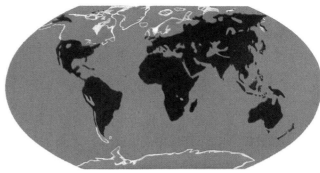

The last Ice Age began about nineteen thousand years ago and lasted for nine thousand years. About a third of the earth's land surface was covered by giant glaciers and a vast ice sheet. Greenland and Antarctica are still covered by ice left behind by previous ice ages.

As they flow, glaciers fill V-shaped river valleys and carve out the valley bottom to form a U shape. The Norwegian sea inlets, or fjords, are valleys that were shaped by glaciers during the last Ice Age. When the ice melted and the sea level rose, these valleys were submerged.

Drumlins are oval humps of rock found near a glacier's end, or snout. They are made from rocks carried by the glacier, molded into shape under the ice, and exposed when the ice melts. Drumlins usually stand in small clusters, or swarms, forming a landscape of low, oval-shaped hills.

How was the Grand Canyon formed?

The Grand Canyon in Arizona is the biggest gorge on earth. It stretches for 217 miles and in places is more than one mile deep. Over millions of years the canyon has been carved out of the rock by the fast-flowing Colorado River.

The vertical cliffs of the Canyon display millions of years of the earth's history. Near the top, the rocks contain fossils of two hundred-million-year-old ferns, insects, and reptiles. At the bottom, rocks are more than two billion years old and show no signs of past life.

18

Shaping the earth

How do waves shape the land?

The sea flings up boulders and pebbles, which wear away soft rocks at the base of cliffs. Waves force air into cracks, splitting the rock. The power of the water eats away caves and arches. Collapsed arches leave pillars of rock, or stacks.

What does acid rain destroy?

Fumes from automobiles and power generating stations mix with rain and make it acidic, like vinegar. When the rain falls, it kills forests and eats away at stone statues.

How does water shape the desert?

Sometimes heavy rain falls in deserts, causing flash floods in deep valleys, or wadis. Like a powerful river, the flash flood eats into the wadi floor, making it deeper.

What are buttes and mesas?

In the deserts of the western United States, horizontal layers of sandstone have been worn away by the wind and water. This erosion forms steep-sided blocks of rock with flat tops called mesas. Further erosion makes narrower blocks called buttes.

Why do rivers meander?

In its early stages a river flows fast and wears away the rocks on its bed and banks. As it flows across flatter land, though, it swings from side to side forming curves, bends, and loops. Sometimes the river breaks through the end of a loop which is cut off by sand and mud, creating an oxbow lake.

How do people shape the earth?

As people use more of the earth's resources, they change the shape of the landscape. They build roads, clear land for farming, and dig huge mines to find coal, gold, and stone. The Bingham Canyon Copper Mine in Utah is 2,625 feet deep and one of the biggest excavations in the world.

How does the wind shape desert rocks?

Desert winds pick up grains of sand and blast them at rocks with great force. The sand grinds the rocks into many unusual shapes. In places the wind bounces sand grains low over the ground. They eat away at the base of rocks, leaving top-heavy mushroom shapes. In the Utah desert, U.S.A., the wind has worn rocks away to leave arches of harder rock.

How do space rocks shape the earth?

Meteorites are huge chunks of rock that fall to earth from outer space. When they hit the earth, they leave giant craters in the ground. One of the most famous meteorite craters is in Arizona. It formed about twenty-seven thousand years ago when a meteorite weighing some two million tons hit the earth. The crater is more than half a mile wide.

Where do waterfalls form?

Waterfalls form where there is an obstacle in a river's path, such as a band of hard rock. The water spills over it and eats away at the softer rock on the other side. As the cliff gets steeper, the water cascades over it in a waterfall. Victoria Falls on the Zambezi River in Africa is one of the world's most dramatic waterfalls. Here the river is nearly a mile wide. It plunges 355 feet over a sheer drop into a narrow gorge below.

More about waterfalls

The highest waterfall in the world is Angel Falls in Venezuela. The water drops 3,212 feet down into a gorge. The Falls were named after an American pilot, Jimmy Angel, who spotted them in 1933 on a flight over the gorge.

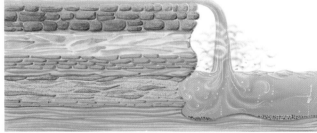

Niagara Falls in the United States and Canada formed about ten thousand years ago. Since then the water has been wearing away the underlying rocks, causing the cliff to collapse again and again. The Falls retreat by more than three feet a year.

A huge white curtain of water and spray often hides the Kaieteur Falls in Guyana from view. Behind the Falls, the water has carved out a large cave which is home to thousands of swallows.

Where are limestone caves found?

Limestone contains the chemical compound calcium carbonate, a constituent of lime. As rain falls on limestone mountains, it reacts with gas in the air and soil, and with the lime, to form a weak acid. Over thousands of years, the acid eats away at the limestone to create a maze of underground tunnels and caves. Stalagmites and stalactites form from the calcium carbonate left behind as drips of water evaporate. Stalagmites grow up from the floor, stalactites hang down from the ceiling.

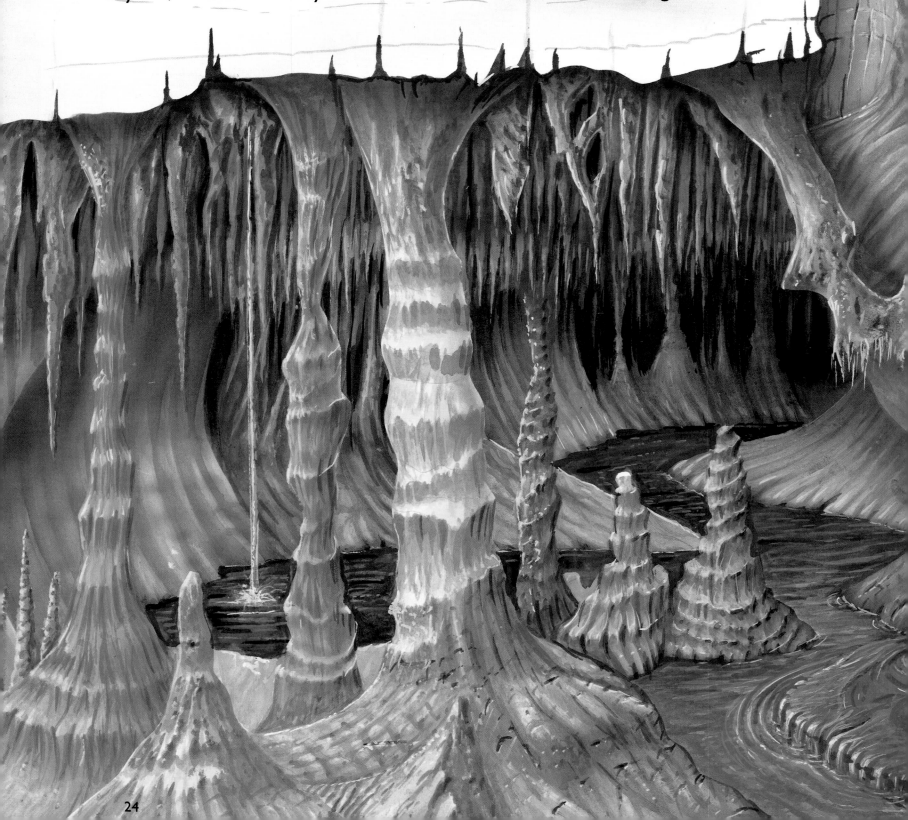

More about caves

During the last Ice Age, huge groups of bears hibernated in caves to escape the bitter cold. The bones of more than thirty thousand cave bears were found in one cave in Austria. They had frozen to death as they slept.

The finest collection of prehistoric cave paintings was found by accident in Lascaux, France. A boy searching for his lost dog discovered hundreds of paintings, drawn about seventeen thousand years ago. They included life-size bulls, mammoths, bison, deer, and horses.

Many cave walls in France and Spain are covered with hand prints. They were made by early people some thirty-five thousand years ago. Some of the hands have fingers missing which were probably lost to frostbite or in a hunting accident.

Rocks and minerals

What are crystals?
Rocks are made up of minerals, formed from natural chemical compounds. There are about three thousand different types of mineral in the earth's crust. As a mineral grows, it may form beautiful shapes called crystals. Quartz is a very common mineral, made up of silicon and oxygen. It often forms milky-white crystals with six sides. Amethyst, a type of quartz, forms purply-blue crystals. These crystals often grow in volcanic rocks.

What is marble?
There are many different kinds of rock. Marble is a type of metamorphic rock. Metamorphic rocks form when other types of rock are pushed down inside the earth and are changed by heat and pressure. Marble is made when limestone is changed in this way. White marble is often used to make statues.

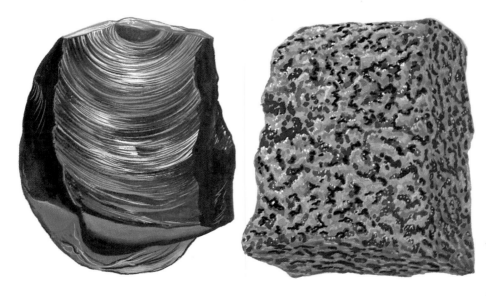

What are igneous rocks?
When a volcano's magma or lava cools, igneous rocks form. Obsidian *(far left)* is a volcanic glass. It forms near to or on the earth's surface when lava freezes quickly. Granite forms beneath the earth's surface and often contains grains of minerals.

What are gemstones?
Gemstones include sapphires, rubies, diamonds, and emeralds. They are the rarest and most beautiful minerals on earth and are very valuable. Gemstones are mined, then cut and polished to make jewelry. Diamond is the hardest mineral known and can be cut only with another diamond. The largest uncut diamond ever found was the Cullinan diamond from South Africa. It was almost the size of a person's fist.

What is flint?

Flint is a variety of chalcedony, a type of quartz. It is usually black or gray and sometimes forms around lumps, called nodules. These can easily be broken into smooth pieces that are sharp enough to cut paper and wood. Prehistoric people used flint to make tools, such as axes, and arrowheads as early as 1.5 million years ago.

What is amber?

Amber is the fossilized sap from pine and fir trees that grew about sixty million years ago. Lumps of amber have been found with the whole bodies of prehistoric spiders and insects trapped inside them.

What are fossils?

Fossils are the remains of prehistoric life, such as the *Archaeopteryx* bird. As its dead body decays, hard minerals replace the original chemical compounds, turning parts of the body to stone.

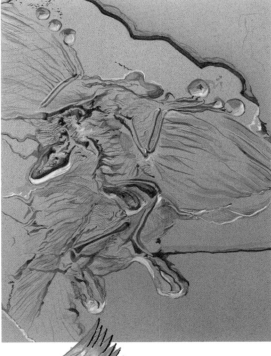

How was coal made?

Millions of years ago, ancient forest plants died and turned into peat. The pressure of rocks on top of the peat squeezed out any water to form coal.

27

What is it like deep under the sea?

Deep under the sea, the landscape is as varied as on dry land. Huge mountains and volcanoes rise up from the sea floor. Vast plains, the flattest places on earth, cover nearly half of the deep-sea floor. Underwater mountain ranges form when ocean plates move apart and magma rises to fill the gap. Where two plates collide, one is pushed under the other and melts back into the earth. This forms a V-shaped trench in the sea floor, which may be nearly seven miles deep.

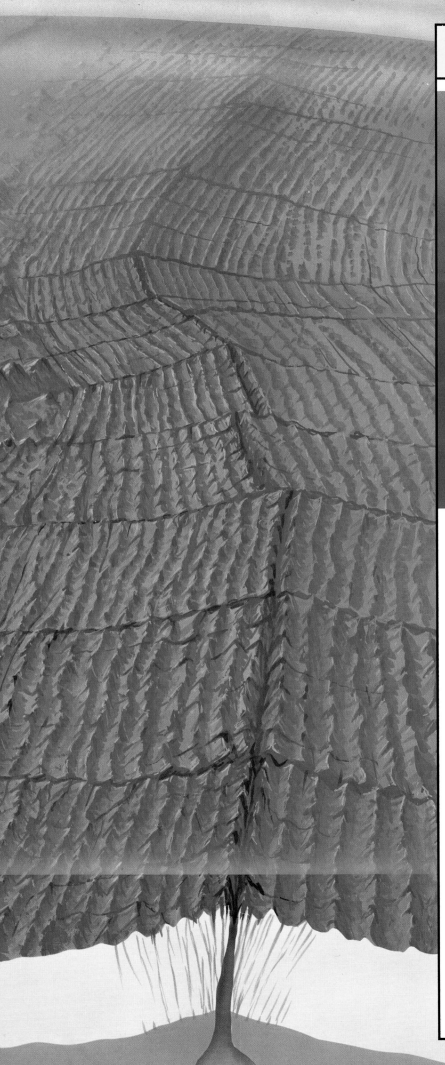

More about the sea

In the past, divers wore heavy helmets and cumbersome suits and boots weighted down with lead. Air pipes connected them to their ship. Modern diving suits, such as WASP, are safer and have their own built-in air supply, which can last for seventy-two hours.

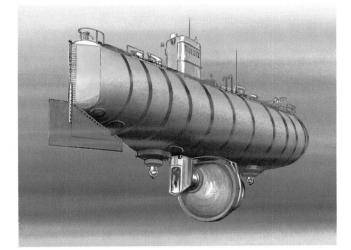

The deepest dive ever made was in 1960 by the bathyscape *Trieste*. A bathyscape is a small submarine, or submersible. It dived 35,800 feet, almost to the bottom of the Marianas Trench in the Pacific Ocean. The crew traveled in a steel sphere with walls five inches thick to prevent their being crushed by the pressure of the water. The descent took four hours and forty-eight minutes.

What are coral atolls?

The Pacific and Indian Oceans are dotted with chains of horseshoe-shaped or circular coral islands called atolls. They enclose deep blue lagoons where the water may be up to 984 feet deep. Atolls started life thousands of years ago as coral reefs. They grew around the base of islands formed by underwater volcanoes. Here the water was warm, sunny, and clear — the ideal conditions for coral. As the volcano sank back into the sea, or as the sea level rose, the coral kept growing to form an atoll.

More about coral

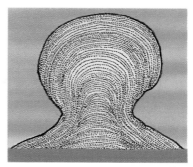

Coral grows a new band of skeleton every day. By counting the bands of seasonal and daily growth on four hundred-million-year-old coral fossils, scientists have calculated that at that time there were four hundred days in a year.

Coral comes in fantastic shapes and sizes. It is built by tiny sea animals called polyps. Polyps use chemical compounds from seawater to build hard skeletons round their soft bodies. When they die, the skeletons remain as coral.

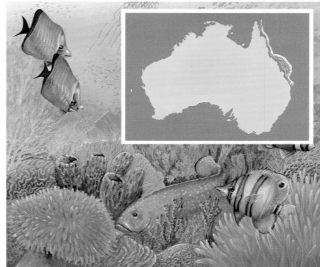

A barrier reef is a long ridge of coral built a little way from the shore. The Great Barrier Reef in Australia is the world's biggest coral reef. It stretches for more than 1,243 miles and has taken at least fifteen million years to build.

How are deltas formed?

As a river reaches the sea, it slows down and deposits some of the load of sediment (stones and mud) collected on its journey. If the load is too big to be carried away by the sea, it forms a muddy plain of new land. This is called a delta. As the sediment settles into large piles at its mouth, the river is forced to branch out and flow around the piles. These smaller streams, called distributaries, create deltas shaped like fans or birds' feet.

More about deltas

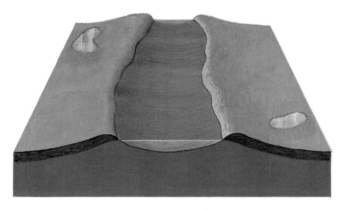

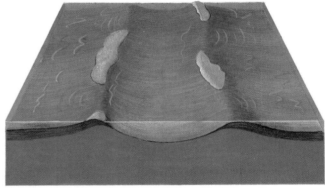

Every year the Mississippi River carries five hundred and fifty million tons of mud and sand toward its delta. As the river sheds its load it builds up ridges, called levees, along its banks. The mud and sand also raise the height of the riverbed, so the river and its levees are higher than the plain around them.

Most people in Bangladesh, in Asia, live by farming on the Ganges delta, which covers an area almost the size of Austria. However, this low-lying area is often hit by fierce storms, and terrible floods sweep over the nearby land. In 1985 over six thousand people drowned as they worked on the delta.

Why is rice grown in terraced fields?

Rice is the main food of over half the world's population. About ninety percent is grown in Asia. Rice needs plenty of water to grow in and is planted in flooded paddy fields.

In some places, such as Indonesia, the rice is grown in terraced paddy fields. These are cut like steps into the hillside. Rice grows well on mountains because there is plenty of rain. Too much rain can wash the soil away, but terraces hold the soil in place.

Weather and climate

What is a rainbow?
If the sun comes out during a shower of rain, a rainbow may form. This is because the raindrops act like tiny prisms and split up the sunlight into the wavelengths or colors that make up white light.

What is lightning?
Lightning is the electricity that builds up in a cloud as water droplets crash into one another. The streak of lightning races to the ground and back. The air it passes through becomes so hot that it expands very quickly, making the noise of thunder.

What are clouds?
Clouds are made up of billions of tiny particles of water or ice. These particles form when warm air rises from the ground and cools.

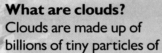

Why is a sunset red?
When the sun is low at sunset its light has a longer way to go to reach the earth. Short blue wavelengths are scattered by gas molecules in the air, leaving the longer red wavelengths to reach the earth and color the sky.

What are monsoons?
In summer, heavy rain pours down on India and other parts of Asia for days on end. This is the monsoon season. A monsoon is a wind system that changes direction with the seasons.

What are snow crystals?
Snow crystals are tiny pieces of ice that join together in a cloud and fall as snowflakes. No two snow crystals are ever the same shape. The shapes form depending on how cold the air is.

What is a dust storm?
In deserts, strong winds whip up sand and dust into big clouds. These dust storms can travel great distances, across many countries.

What causes dew and frost?
When the ground cools at night, it cools the air above it. At a certain point, water vapor in the air condenses (turns to liquid) and forms droplets, or dew. Below freezing point, the dew freezes and becomes frost.

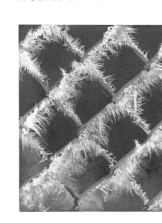

What are hurricanes?

Hurricanes are huge, whirling storms that form over tropical seas. Air is heated by the sea, spirals upward, and cools to form a great wheel of storm clouds and driving rain, over three hundred miles wide. Howling winds blow at up to one hundred and ninety miles per hour.

Hurricanes cause great damage if they reach land. They whip up huge waves, flatten crops, and destroy buildings. One of the worst hurricanes ever, Hurricane David, hit the West Indies in 1979 and killed more than one thousand people.

More about storms

In the center of a hurricane there is a surprisingly calm area about twenty miles wide, called the eye. Here there is blue sky and very little wind. As the eye passes over land the storm weakens.

Tornadoes are funnel-shaped storms which twist down from storm clouds. They are much smaller than hurricanes but much more violent. Tornadoes are common in the American Midwest. They bounce over the land causing enormous damage.

Waterspouts are similar to tornadoes but happen over the sea. Swirling winds suck the water up into great funnels, which may be more than half a mile high. Waterspouts are strong enough to smash ships apart if they collapse.

Where do rain forests grow?

Hot, steamy rain forests grow along the equator in South America, Africa, and Southeast Asia. They cover less than a tenth of the earth but are home to some two thirds of all the species of animals and plants. The rain forests are always warm, and it rains almost every day.

The world's greatest rain forest grows along the banks of the Amazon River in Brazil. It contains more than sixteen hundred species of bird and more than a million species of insect. Its trees produce rubber, nuts, timber and medicines.

More about the rain forests

Rain forest trees are arranged in layers. The tallest trees grow to 295 feet tall. Below them is a green canopy of treetops, where most of the animals and birds live. Little sunlight reaches the forest floor, where there is a covering of rotting leaves that nourish the trees.

Each year an area of rain forest twice the size of Austria is cut down, and trees are burned to make space for buildings and farms. Soon the rain forests may disappear altogether. This would leave thousands of rare animals homeless in a wasteland. Also, burning trees release gases that make the earth warmer. This could melt the ice at the poles and flood low-lying countries.

What are deserts?

Deserts are very dry places, with less than ten inches of rain a year. The Atacama Desert in Chile had no rain for four hundred years from 1570 to 1971. Deserts may be very hot in the day, with temperatures up to 136°F. At night, though, the temperature may drop to below freezing. Not all deserts are sandy. Some are covered with rock and gravel. The Sahara is the world's largest desert, covering about a third of Africa. It also has the highest sand dunes, some towering up to fourteen hundred feet high.

42

More about deserts

Despite the heat and lack of water, many plants survive in the desert. Giant saguaro cacti in the American deserts can weigh up to ten tons. About nine tons of this weight is water stored in the stem.

The desert can sometimes become a carpet of many colors. Huge numbers of desert flowers suddenly bloom as soon as it rains, making the most of the rare supply of water.

Thirsty desert travelers sometimes see a tempting oasis of water close by. As they get nearer, though, the oasis disappears. This is an optical illusion called a mirage. In the desert, warm air near the ground bends light coming from the sky. This creates the image of a pool of water at ground level.

Why is the Arctic so cold?

The Arctic is the area around the North Pole and the Antarctic is the area around the South Pole. There is no land in the Arctic, just the frozen Arctic Ocean. The Arctic is cold all year round, with temperatures often below −22°F. At the edges of the Arctic Ocean the sea is littered with icebergs.

At the equator, the sun's rays hit the earth directly, with the full force of their heat. At the poles, though, the rays hit the ground at angles. They are much weaker because they are so spread out, making both poles the coldest places in the world.

More about the Arctic

For centuries, Inuits living in the Arctic have made homes out of the snow around them. They cut the snow into blocks and build these into the walls of an igloo. The snow traps heat so well that the inside of the igloo is always warm.

The Norwegian explorer Roald Amundsen became the first man to reach the South Pole. He arrived at the South Pole on December 14, 1911. In 1926 he became the first man to have seen both poles when he flew over the North Pole in an airship.

In June and July the sun never sets at the North Pole, and at night the "midnight sun" shines. The South Pole, meanwhile, has twenty-four-hour darkness. During December and January the reverse happens. This process occurs because the earth tilts as it orbits the sun.

INDEX

AN ILEX BOOK
Created and produced by Ilex Publishers Limited
29-31 George Street, Oxford, OX1 2AJ

Main illustrations by Mike Saunders/Jillian Burgess Illustration
Other illustrations by Mike Saunders, Brian Watson, Jack Pelling/Linden
Artists Ltd and Amanda Deadman/Hardlines